Praise for

Gratitude Bump: Four Steps to Joy and Success

"What a great read! The message was so well written and it really speaks to readers of all ages."
–*Erika Yanez, P.R. and Communications Specialist*

"Ms. Mayer's book may be small and simple, but it opens up like a gift at Christmas from someone who knew exactly what to give you...In bite-sized pieces she explains how this [method] improves not only your life but those around you...This book will make a great gift book to your friends, family, and work colleagues. Keep one on your coffee table, because the few minutes that it takes to read will create a fun and robust conversation." –*Larry Hamilton, M.A., L.M.F.T.*

"I'm sold! I would definitely recommend this book to my colleagues, family, friends, etc.!"
–*Monica Orbegoso, Career Development & Social Skills Instructor*

"This gift book is an accessible guide to instilling the importance of gratitude...Teaching this trait from an early age will help children develop a positive mindset critical to mental health."
–*Virginia Valerio-Lambert, Founder and Artistic Director, Art Integration Education*

"This book made me feel warm and fuzzy – much like cuddling an actual puppy. The content is gentle but powerful, reminding readers that joy, connection, and emotional well-being can come from the simplest interactions." –*Edi Matsumoto, Nurse Practitioner, Author, and Artist*

"...a fabulous book EVERY person will benefit from, and especially the younger generations who are yearning for direction on success and finding happiness in this upside-down world...having a pleasurable, easy, understandable, and timeless formula backed by science where the benefits are infinite..." –*Ingrid A. Otteson, Award-Winning Sales & Marketing Professional and Mother of four*

"I enjoyed the simplicity of the steps and the reasoning of each. They are applicable to and can easily be understood by adults and children." –*Audrey Kitayama, Educator and Parent of Carmel Cotillions graduate*

ISBN 979-8-218-86927-4

Gratitude Bump® The term Gratitude Bump is registered with the USPTO and is protected by United States Trademark law.

Published by Carmel Cotillions, LLC, dba Network for Impact

Printed in the United States of America. This book was written without the use of artificial intelligence except for standard spell check features in Microsoft Word, and with photo editing features in Microsoft Word.

Thank you, Reader, for preparing your children (and yourself!) for a better life. It brings me joy to help you parent well. –MGM

Thank you to our children, who grew up to be wonderful people in spite of what life threw at them, and to my husband, who keeps trying every day. –MGM

Dear Reader,

Here is your pocket guide to achieving joy and success in all areas of your life, and to training your children to do the same. Gratitude research has tested various gratitude interventions (assignment tasks), measuring their short- and long-term impacts on relationships, productivity, mental and physical health, academic success, and even growing wealth. The Gratitude Bump® method is crafted to maximize these benefits by narrowing the most impactful interventions to one Four Step process.

Your grandmother was right. Giving a proper Thank You isn't just good for the other person; it is good for YOU. On the following pages, you will find the best form of self-care: creating your own Gratitude Bump - simply, repeatedly, and infinitely. While global levels of stress and anxiety grow, psychologists are concluding with increasing frequency that mental health treatments should include gratitude assignments.

To best equip your children for their futures, start training them now. Keep reading to improve your life - and the lives of your children - with every written and spoken Thank You.

Gratitude Bump

Four Steps to Joy and Success

Megan G. Mayer

Network for Impact

Contents

The Gratitude Bump

improves your life in **every** way.

Research shows that **every time** you express gratitude, you improve your

- Physical Health
- Mental Health
- Financial Wealth
- Academic Performance
- Professional Success
- Relationship Satisfaction

Every area of your life **improves** each time you express gratitude.

Training your children to express gratitude improves **their** lives.

Think of it as a

Gratitude Bump

that bumps up your
mood,
productivity,
and relationships
every time you
express gratitude.

Each expression of gratitude creates another

Gratitude Bump.

Which means the
improvement
to your life is
theoretically...

infinite.

A Simple Formula

The large body of gratitude research
reveals that using Four Steps in your

Thank You

maximizes your

Gratitude Bump.

Practicing these Four Steps every day builds the habit of expressing gratitude and equips you for a successful future.

While you benefit from expressing gratitude, so do those you thank.

They like knowing you

received their gift,

noticed their gesture,

or appreciated their kind words.

Gift givers **love** knowing you received and enjoyed their gift.

Everyone **loves**

when children say Thank You.

Whether you write or speak
your gratitude,

use the same Four Steps to
create your

Gratitude Bump.

Express your gratitude in Four Steps

1. the words *"Thank You"*

2. the Person's *Name*

3. for *What* you are thanking them

4. *Why* you are grateful

Step One

"Thank You"

Saying the words

"*Thank You*"

is an important part of expressing gratitude.

The words *"Thank You"* attribute your gratitude toward the person responsible for the gift, gesture, or words.
They make clear that you give them credit.

People enjoy receiving credit for what they give, do, and say.

People often forget to say the words

"Thank You"

when thanking someone.

Depending on the rest of the words
shared, the expression of gratitude
might still be clear.

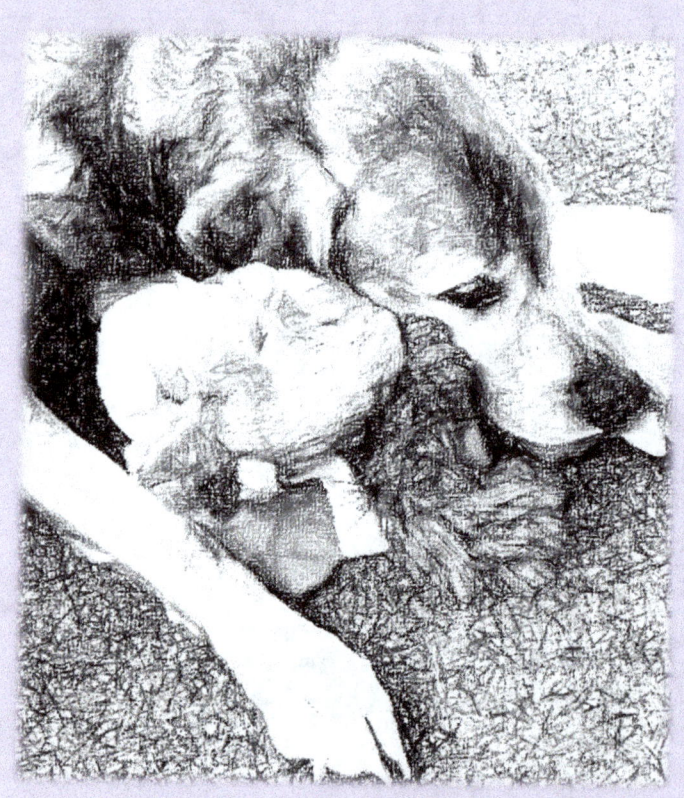

More often, the
person thanked
feels unappreciated
and the thank you
sounds
disingenuous.

Including the words

"Thank You"

makes your intentions clear.

"Thank You"

is like the

Headline for an article

or the

Label for a box.

It clearly identifies your message.

⚬ Step Two ⚬

The Person's Name

Just like saying the words *"Thank You"*

clarifies What you are saying,

stating the

Person's

Name

clarifies that you are

thanking **them**

specifically.

People enjoy hearing their own

Name.

When you say someone's *Name*,

their attention increases.

Using their *Name*

speaks to their brain's limbic system.

Think of the limbic system as the

Puppy Brain.

When you say a puppy's *Name…*

they

- turn to look at you
- perk their ears to listen to you
- sit up a little straighter
- stand to attention
- anticipate something *good.*

Using their *Name* in your

Thank You causes the person to

- pay closer attention

- hear your words more positively

- make a positive association with *You.*

Your expression of gratitude is more personal and more sincere when you use their *Name.*

To magnify the impact of your words and communicate your gratitude fully, add positive

- eye contact
- body language
- facial expressions

The most powerful word in any language is your Name.

(to paraphrase Dale Carnegie)

Step Three

The What

A *Thank You* should always mention in detail *What* you are thankful for.

Thank you

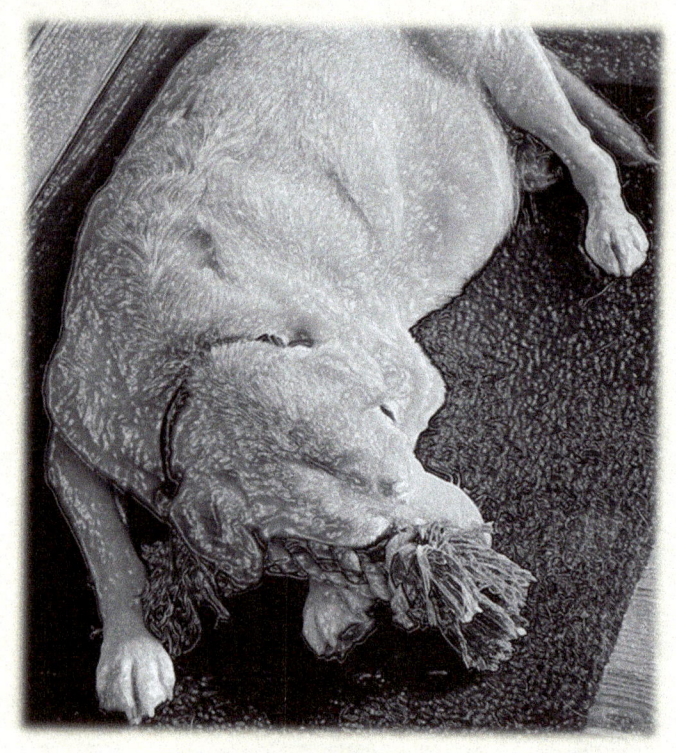

"Thanks
for the gift,"
is not
as powerful as

"Thank You for the toy rope
for our dog Naboo."

Saying **"Thank You,"** while walking

away from your driver, is not as powerful as

- facing your driver
- while in the car
- smiling
- saying...

"Thank You for driving me home."

Details ensure the giver knows you received their gift. Telling them you received their gift is especially helpful with online shopping or gifts of money.

❧ Abstract Gifts ❧

When thanking someone for

kind words,

be specific

about what was encouraging or

helpful to you.

Abstract Gifts

When thanking for a

gesture

or **support,**

give details about what they did
that was helpful.

Abstract Gifts

Rather than

vague generalities,

give specific

Details

in your

Thank You.

Detailing

What

you received

makes the

person feel

appreciated.

43

Instead of *"Thank you for..."*

- the gift
- the money
- what you said
- your support
- your help
- the book

Say *"Thank you for..."*

- the toy snake for our dog Naboo
- the $25 Visa gift card
- recognizing my long hours
- promoting my idea in the meeting
- helping me load my car
- the copy of <u>The World of Bats</u>

Step Four

The Why

The *Why* is the real magic in

creating your

Gratitude Bump.

Share *Why* you appreciate what they did, said, or gave you.

Dive deep into your feelings of gratitude.

Consider the

- significance of the gift to you
- time and effort the giver invested
- thoughtfulness of the giver
- story behind the gift
- impact of the gift, words, or gesture

The more *Details* you share about *Why* you are appreciative, the bigger your **Gratitude Bump.**

Sharing *Details* on *Why* you are grateful pleases their *Puppy Brain.* They feel appreciated, effective, and generally good about themselves. It also makes them feel good about

You.

Articulating your *Why* in *Detail* pleases Your *Puppy Brain.*

It improves your

- brain chemistry
- brain activity
- mood
- relationships

Sharing *Details* with your gift giver is good

for them - but it is better for *You.*

The **Gratitude Bump** is the

best form of self-care.

The deeper your reflection and clearer your expression of gratitude, the more powerful is your Gratitude Bump.

A Healthy Habit

Pamper yourself every day by
creating your own

Gratitude Bump.

Practice Makes Perfect

Find daily opportunities to say

Thank You.

Teachers • Contractors • Coworkers • Store Clerks
Military Service Members • Carpool Drivers • Clients
Food Servers • Volunteers • Postal Workers • Babysitters
Deliverers • Librarians • Supervisors • Neighbors
Camp Leaders • Cashiers • Coaches • Healthcare Providers

and especially *Family & Friends*

Say *Thank You* often to model it for your

children and to create your own

Gratitude Bump.

You win with every Thank You!

Expressing gratitude creates a

Gratitude Bump

that improves every area of your life.

Training your children to create their own

Gratitude Bump

equips them for a
joyful and successful life.

Thank You

Name

What

Why

Four Steps create your

Gratitude Bump

Thank You,
Reader,
for reading this book and supporting
my message.
I love helping you prepare your
children (and yourself!) for a better
life. It brings me great joy to help
you parent well.

Gratitude

Thank you to all who brought this small book to life. Editors Diane, Doug, Edi, Erika, Fred, Jeannie, Kita, Larry, Lauren, Marianna, Monica, Rosaleen, Tetyana, and Virginia contributed broad perspectives and great questions to make this message effective in a short format. Ingrid A. Otteson was uniquely energetic in her support and feedback. Jeannie Thorndike, Ph.D., L.M.F.T., deserves special posthumous recognition for assigning a gratitude task that brought light to our lives well before research on the task was published. Larry Hamilton, M.A., L.M.F.T., skillfully guided our family for decades as what our son called, "our assistant dad." My husband and children continue to support me in sharing our story of gratitude, for which I am most appreciative, and our extended family, friends, and neighbors deserve a thank you for many years of patience and grace with all of us. I am additionally grateful for the unconditional love and joy of sweet dogs.

Photography

Page 51, 55, and 65 photographed by Monica F. Orbegoso. Subject is Naboo at Carmel Beach in California.

All others photographed by the author's family members. Subjects are Dippie, Naboo, Lando, Hobbes, Appa, and Momo.

All photos were treated using Microsoft Word photo editing tools.

Gift box pencil sketch drawn by Doug Mayer and treated using Microsoft Word photo editing tools.

Research

Since the 1990s, Gratitude research has quickly grown as an academic field of study. The extensive and growing body of research that tested how gratitude interventions support all areas of our lives is too long to fit in this book. This book boils down the research I read (without using artificial intelligence) to the most succinct summary of the behaviors that will maximize the benefits from practicing and expressing gratitude – the Gratitude Bump®.

Visit www.network4impact.net or use this QR code for your:

- Four Step Gratitude Bump Card
- Gratitude Bump Research List
- Gratitude Worksheet
- *Plus more!*

Coming soon...

Gratitude Bump

The Science and Story of Creating Joy and Success

A story of how gratitude research created the Gratitude Bump®, told through a family's journey overcoming brain injury.

About the Author

Megan G. Mayer is a retired attorney and mother of three who writes, speaks, and trains on professional communication and networking skills. She developed her Gratitude Bump® and Polite Argument® methods while raising her children after her husband's brain injury. The book clubs she created to teach her children respectful, logical argument and effective listening, formed what is now the Polite Argument method. She founded Carmel Cotillions to finish her youngest child's manners training. When crafting this curriculum, she discovered the world of gratitude research, and created her Gratitude Bump method. The research convinced her that these are not soft skills; they are survival skills.

She has published and spoken on economics, law, leadership, networking, and parenting, and is featured in *Insider*, *The Orange County Register*, *The UCLA Journal of Gender and Law*, *Medical Board of California Newsletter*, *Family Practice Management*, *Monterey Herald Health Matters Magazine*, and *The Carmel Pinecone*. Megan lives in California with her husband and two dogs. When she is not writing or walking the dogs, she speaks to parent and professional audiences, and volunteers at local programs for youth professional development. You can learn more about her work at www.network4impact.net.